Mind OF MINE

POEMS OF LOVE, LOSS, AND FRIENDSHIP

ELIJAH B. CHAVEZ

Mind of Mine

Copyright © 2024 by Elijah B. Chavez.

All rights reserved. No part of this publication may be reproduced, distributed, or transmitted in any form or by any means, including photocopying, recording, or other electronic or mechanical methods, without the written consent of the publisher. The only exceptions are for brief quotations included in critical reviews and other noncommercial uses permitted by copyright law.

MILTON & HUGO L.L.C.
4407 Park Ave., Suite 5
Union City, NJ 07087, USA

Website: *www. miltonandhugo.com*
Hotline: *1- 888-778-0033*
Email: *info@miltonandhugo.com*

Ordering Information:
Quantity sales. Special discounts are granted to corporations, associations, and other organizations. For more information on these discounts, please reach out to the publisher using the contact information provided above.

Library of Congress Control Number:	2024907849	
ISBN-13:	979-8-89285-077-3	[Paperback Edition]
	979-8-89285-079-7	[Hardback Edition]
	979-8-89285-078-0	[Digital Edition]

Rev. date: 06/18/2024

"A heart-shaped face I can't let go, and a heart worth the wait."
- SOFT

THE

POETICAL WORKS

OF

ELIJAH B. CHAVEZ.

Dedication

I hope you smile while you read this; it was for you.

Acknowledgments

This work would not be possible without the encouragements and effort of my family. I cannot express how much their support has meant to me. I have never been much of a writer, and so when I expressed an interest in publishing something, it came as a shock to everyone. When it was revealed, the work would be poetry that almost made their eyes pop. Regardless, they pushed me to follow through with my goal. I am glad they did, and I hope you, the reader, are too. While I don't expect anything here to be profound or life-changing; I hope some of the writings make you smile. If that was accomplished, then I did what I set out to do. So lastly, I'd like to acknowledge anyone who has read this work. Thank you.

TABLE OF CONTENTS

Dedication ix

Acknowledgments xi

LETTERS OF LOVE.

You 3

Never before 4

Beauty 5

Beauty of the tides 6

Sweet little smirk 7

Attributes 9

Plus, one 10

I'm not saying 11

Destin 12

I have 13

With 14

My Promise 15

What I would do? 16

Soft 18

Pure 20

Uncommon 22

Ways to say I love you 24

Foley 26

The word 28

Should you 30

Later 32

Only one 34

What is it? 36

I Love 38

If I could do it again 40

The Dream 42

Secret Smile... 44

When.. 46

Question...47

Letters 48

I could 49

If you 51

To My Future Forever.....................................52

LETTERS OF LONGING.

I Shouldn't..57

About a year 58

Her 60

Was It?...62

If I could 64

Need To Say.. 66

Just Say 68

Where do I go?...69

I Want..70

Out of reach 72

Goodbye Dear..74

You Said... 77

One thing...79

I Will 80

Memories...81

Leave me in the morning................................. 82

Leave you in the morning................................ 83

LETTERS OF FAMILY, FRIENDS, & LOSS.

Grey 87

Mama 89

Papa...91

Still holding On...93

Farewell..95

My memories 96

Friends... 98

Time.. 100

LETTERS OF FAITH.

Follow 103

Faith.. 104

The Path.. 107

I See.. 109

About the Author.. 111

LETTERS OF LOVE.

You

Your soft, warm smile;
Your gentle, caring touch;
The notes in your voice;
That I cherish so much.

Your kind, sweet soul;
Your radiance hazel eyes;
Your energy and purpose;
Driven, a true prize.

Your light tan skin;
Your beautiful flowing hair;
The way your eyes capture mine;
Trapped like a snare.

Your large, loving heart;
Your giving, lovely soul;
Your perfect imperfections;
With you, my heart is whole.

I don't know how to say this;
Standing face to face;
Because when I'm around you;
I'm stuck there by your grace.

And so, I write to tell you,
I couldn't love you more.
Then, again, I thought that yesterday;
And I've been wrong before.

Never before

I have never been in love before;
This I surely know.
I have never felt this way before;
This longing in my soul.
I have never cared for one before;
For what they do and feel.
I have never wanted to be before;
Somebody's place to heal.
I have never wanted to know before;
Someone down to their heart.
I have never felt this empty before;
Torn when we're apart.
I have never loved so purely before;
So honest and so true.
I have never been in love before;
Til the day that I met you.

Beauty

The Beauty of your smile;
My eyes are blessed to behold.
The Beauty of your heart;
My feelings for you untold.

The Beauty of your trust;
You see the best in all.
The Beauty of your strength;
You get up each time you fall.

The Beauty of your thoughts;
Do not let them go unheard.
The Beauty of your voice;
I hang onto every word.

The Beauty of your resolve;
Tough, you push on through.
The Beauty of your dreams;
You work till they come true.

The Beauty of your passion;
My soul cannot unsee.
The Beauty of your love;
I cherish what's given to me.

The Beauty of your life;
Your happiness, it shows.
And blessed am I to see;
How far your Beauty goes.

Beauty of the tides

Beautiful as the tides at sunset.
As strong as winds at storm.
Striking in your elegance.
Stunning in your form.

Your soul I have loved forever.
This life and all before.
No matter the time or distance,
My feelings for you are pure.

Eyes, the color of amber.
Hair, long brown and free.
I have not much to give you;
But I give you fully me.

You smile when our eyes meet;
And I can't help but smile too.
I don't know what you see in me;
But I see everything in you.

My love, my present, my future;
My wife, my heart, my truth.
I cared before I knew you;
I've loved you since my youth.

So, take with you this one fact.
Something to hold as true.
In every life imaginable;
I could love only you.

Sweet little smirk

Sweet little smirk;
With lips, I can't forget.
Hair in a bun;
Bandanna to catch sweat.

Your life is still vibrant;
Opportunistic and free, it's true.
I thought mine was over;
Til the day that I met you.

Your tongue-and-cheek jokes;
Your love for those around.
Your gentle, teaching nature;
Your beauty knows no bounds.

Your lousy taste in music;
I'll forgive you for that here.
Cause I'll listen to anything;
So long as you are near.

Your passionate love for swimming;
Your drive carries on.
Your discipline and dedication;
Makes you in your life strong.

Your cute button nose;
Your soft, hazel eyes.
So gentle to look at;
I can speak to them no lies.

I stand here and watch you;
And thank God that we met.
For where would I be;
If not caught in your net.

Attributes

Brow the color of acorns;
The color of trees and sand.
Blinding in their beauty;
As pure as untouched land.

Messy as a junk drawer;
Different shades of brown.
Perfectly unkept;
Long, full, and unbound.

Crooked trying to hide it;
Tight but shining past.
Hide it as you try;
But pure as shining glass.

Large, strong, and innocent;
Earnest, loving full.
What first I truly noticed;
What made me fall for you.

Your eyes, your hair, your smile;
Your heart, so pure and true.
Everything I've listed;
What makes you fully you.

Lost, entranced, and captured;
Held there by your presence.
And so, to you, I offer;
My heart and it's surrenderince.

Plus, one

I had never stood a chance;
And I never wanted to.
For all the time I've searched in life,
I've searched in vain till you.

I knew you when I met you;
And you knew me just the same.
There were no awkward moments;
No moments not in frame.

We connected at our meeting;
Like lightning to the thunder.
You healed me without trying;
And pulled me from asunder.

I'm supposed to be the strong one;
The one to lead and guide.
I lost my way in weakness;
You helped restore pride.

You did it without thinking;
It's just a natural part of you.
I've loved you from our meeting;
And I hope you felt it too.

Heartstrings that bind and hold us;
Our feelings outshine the sun.
I will love you truly and always.
Forever a day; plus, one.

I'm not saying

I'm not saying that you're perfect,
Because I know that it's not true.
But if perfection cracked a mirror,
Its reflection would be you.

I'm not saying that you're beautiful,
Because I know you hate to hear it.
But if you were a flowing river,
I'd find peace by standing near it.

I'm not saying that you're wonderful,
Because I know that's hard to prove.
But if the world were budding flowers,
Then red roses would be you.

I'm not saying that I love you,
Because it seems too soon to say.
But I know the thing that scares me most,
Is to live without you one more day.

Destin

Everlasting is your beauty;
With a flawless, righteous heart.
Our fates were intertwined;
I was destined to love you from the start.

Matchup made in heaven,
At least, it seems that way.
Tied together since our meeting,
Made to treasure you more each day.

Enchanted and enduring,
This love that we both share.
And I could never imagine,
My life without you here.

Lovely is your presence,
And sweet is your voice.
Melodic is your cadence,
Your sound is my first choice.

You laugh when I say that,
My heart's always known what's true,
That even before we'd meet,
My soul's always been waiting for you.

I have

I have loved you in the mornings;
In the days before I knew.
Before you ever crossed my way,
I have loved you through and through.

I have loved you in the evenings;
Searching in life for you.
On the day and moment, we first met;
I knew love to be true.

I will love you in the nighttime;
In the darkness in times of woe.
From here to forever, we shall endeavor;
I will love you; you'll always know.

With

With these hands,
I promise to hold you;
And be your steady stand.

With these arms,
I promise to carry you;
And be your place to land.

With this mouth,
I promise to tell you;
I Love you more each day.

In this heart,
I promise to keep you;
Even after I pass away.

My Promise

My hands are rough;
But you hold them anyway.
My life was tough;
But you took away all those days.

My heart was hard;
But you chiseled away at it.
My trust was on guard;
But you had enough room to fit.

I am glad that you didn't;
Leave and give up on me.
Because without you here,
I don't know where I'd be.

From our first encounter,
With each passing hour,
I'm so thankful I met you;
And our love got to flower.

So, hear what I say next;
And know that it's honest.
I'll love you forever;
And dear, that is my promise.

What I would do?

I would learn how to paint;
Just to paint you.
I would learn how to sing;
So, you'd hear my heart tune.

I would learn how to write;
And compose you a song.
I would learn what is right;
To never do you wrong.

I would climb the highest mountain;
To confirm the truth, I know.
That even the world's beauty;
Is just a shadow to your soul.

I would swim the deepest oceans;
And touch the bottom floor,
So that I could certainly say;
My love's deeper all the more.

I would fly as high as possible;
Get to space and beyond.
Just so I can validate;
Your eyes outshine the sun.

I wish I could do for you;
All that I've said and more.
Be a perfect connecting balance;
Like an ocean to the shore.

And so, I'll do what I can;
So, you can know for true.
In all my days, I'll show you ways;
My love will shine for you.

Soft

Soft, sweet, and glinting,
Your beautiful brown eyes.
Light dusting freckles,
I count to pass the time

Thick auburn hair
Flowing long and straight.
A heart-shaped face I can't let go,
And a heart worth the wait.

I'll stay here right beside you,
And start forever now.
I'll thank God deep in prayer,
That I met you here somehow.

I'll look when you're not looking,
And be all-struck by your side.
I can't help but favor your gestures,
And the smiles you try to hide.

A laugh I'll always remember,
A voice I'll never forget.
To dance with you in December,
And reminisce on how we met.

I smile, and I stumble,
Talking when you're around.
Feeling lost in conversation;
Lost yet truly found.

How do you pull it from me;
This feeling deep inside?
I've never felt not once before;
Now, something I can't hide.

So, stay here with me once more;
Don't leave me all alone.
Because there's no place or feeling of grace;
Without you, there's no home.

Pure

Your cold, red nose;
And soft, warm eyes.
Thick, full lips;
Smile, a true prize.

You're as pure as the snow;
And as pretty as fall.
Consuming as the rain;
My heart, you have it all.

I could search for a century;
A millennium or two.
From beginning to end,
And I'd still love just you.

The way we lock gazes;
Our souls intertwined.
I reach for your heart;
On meeting you had mine.

Perfect in your passions;
Beauty in your resolve.
You reach for the heavens;
Every question is to be solved.

As for me, I just watch you;
Standing by your side.
All you want, I want too.
In my chest is where you reside.

My hearts out on my sleeve now;
Bearer out free and true.
And a better man I am today;
All because I have met you.

And so, I will say it once more;
Again, for you to know.
I love you here and always;
And each day, my love will grow.

Uncommon

As rare as desert rain;
With eyes that shine so true.
Bunned up messy hair;
Ready to try all that you do.

A fighter in more than spirit;
A lover without pause.
Always ready to push hard;
And fight for a good cause.

You give soft smirks so freely;
But smiles, I rarely see.
Although I've caught one or two;
Locking eyes, you with me.

You have a strong pulling presence;
You draw me by your side.
And when I'm right there next to you;
There's nothing I can hide.

You whisper that you love me;
And I love you all the more.
So, know my love, my feelings;
Won't change if rich or poor.

For I would give up all the wealth,
That one man can possess.
And I would pass with flying colors,
Every trial, trick, or test.

Cause feeling what I feel for you,
Is more than just a fling.
And burning in my pocket now,
Is our forever ring.

Ways to say I love you

How many different ways,
Can I say that I love you?
How many different ways,
Can I show my is heart is true?

How many different times,
Can I tell you from my soul.
That you're the only one for me;
How many times until you'll know?

Actions, intentions, words;
All of which I'll say and do.
To keep you near and show you dear,
That my love for you is true.

Passion, drive, and meaning;
I will always put forth my best.
To show to you my feelings are true;
And they'll never falter or rest.

More than all the stars in the sky;
Til forever a day and on.
Until my single last breath;
And even after I'm gone.

I will love you until the sun goes dark,
And I will love you in the darkness.
Till the end of the world and after,
I will love you there regardless.

If we had different bodies,
If I were born blind.
I would find the soul that's yours,
And I'd love you for all time.

I would know you by your smile,
By your laugh or by your breathing,
I would know you by your walk,
By any metric, test, or feeling.

I would hear your voice if deft,
I would see your beauty blind.
I would feel your heart if numb,
I would know you to be mine.

Should I disappear and wander;
A decade, one or two.
Should you think that you've changed at all,
I'd still know you through and through.

So, know now that I love you;
And my love will stand the time.
However, you want me to say it;
I am yours, and you are mine.

Foley

They say that love is foolish;
Ridiculous, absurd.
That there's no way to measure it;
That it's only just a word.

And maybe what they say is true;
Maybe they are right.
Cause love seems insufficient;
For this feeling, I hold tight.

They say love sometimes falters;
Sometimes it goes away.
So, what I feel cannot be love;
Cause forever it will stay.

They say love's fake and foley;
It's just a chemical we feel.
And if that's true, what I have for you;
Is not love, if that's real.

So many songs and poems;
Speak of heartbreak, love untrue.
And so, I know with certainty;
It's not love that I feel for you.

For what I hold inside of me;
This burning in my chest.
That keeps me warm up on cold nights;
And makes me try my best.

No rhymes, no words, no rhythm;
No sentence structure made.
Could ever convey, to my heart's dismay,
What I'll feel till I'm unmade.

This scorching passionate feeling;
This aching, longing hold.
You have on me; I cannot see;
How words can have it told.

So, I won't say here that I love you;
Because the word it doesn't fit.
Instead, what I'll do when I'm with you;
Is let passion for you emit.

The word

I used to think there were only;
Two types of love in life.
The kind you live or die for;
A balance of beauty and strife.

But here with you, I know;
What I feel for you is more;
While the world may stay the same,
With you, it seems less dour.

Because knowing that you're out there,
It keeps me uplifted;
Meeting you and knowing you;
In my life, I've been gifted.

I don't know how to describe,
Just what I feel for you.
But gone are the burdens,
I carried and never knew.

Washed away forgotten,
From the moment we crossed paths,
Is it love or infatuation?
Or have I lost my mind at last?

To say to you I love you,
It is such a flimsy term;
People say it all the time;
Yet, they can't feel my passion burn.

The word seems insufficient,
For how our souls connect;
The feelings and emotions;
Over-joyous and perfect.

I used to think there were only;
Two types of love in life;
The kind you live or die for;
A balance of beauty and strife.

I realize now I'm wrong,
Feeling both and so much more;
Ready to live and die;
And open all of life's new doors.

So, I'll tell you that I love you,
Since that's the word we have,
Just know that it means so much more,
Than, any word I've ever said.

Should you

I want to make memories with you,
for every place that we visit.
And every part of your life,
well, I don't want to miss it.

There is something to be said,
about finding what we've found.
From the moment that I saw you,
my love to you was bound.

And tired am I of living,
My life all alone.
I didn't know what I was missing,
But when I met you, I was home.

I'm tied to your memory,
I just can't forget.
All the things that you've said to me,
Or the day that we had met.

Your laughter and your smile,
The sparkle in your eyes.
You're lilting, sweet voice,
And the soft of your goodbyes.

Natural and beautiful,
Determined and free.
As close to perfect,
As a person can be.

I smile when I see you,
I grin when you talk.
I listen when you're speaking,
I stride slower when we walk.

I want to stay here next to you,
Not just today but in life.
And should you want it too, my heart,
I want you for my wife.

Later

My heart fell for you instantly,
My mind realized it later.
My path had altered; you walking in,
My future was all the greater.

I loved just being around you,
I loved the way you looked at me.
And then there started little changes,
I started smiling more, you see.

It was rapture being near you,
Euphoric, elated bliss.
I felt somber when we parted,
It was your presence that I'd miss.

You were tough, energetic, and funny,
You smiled and laughed so free.
And after seeing your eyes light up,
I wanted their reason to be me.

We started talking a little longer,
I wanted to know about your life.
And this was something new to me,
These feelings, sharp as a knife.

When we would finish our conversations,
I couldn't hang up the phone.
Because I'd go from hearing your voice,
To being alone there in my home.

You made me try harder,
I'd plan the future out at night.
Each time I'd fall a little farther,
I'd want you more come morning light.

And then a day had finally passed,
When I realized something new.
I hadn't seen it happening,
But I somehow fell for you.

You see, it wasn't supposed to be this way,
But I guess my soul's a traitor.
Because my heart fell for you instantly,
Only my mind realized it later.

Only one

I've loved only once;
In all of my life.
Not a single time with others;
Had I ever felt right.

I have seen others beautiful;
Some powerful and some bright.
But never has one once drawn me,
Like a moth to the light.

I have talked to the funny;
The insightful and the rude.
But the voice inside my chest;
Only cries out for you.

I have admired a multitude;
Been fascinated by some.
But my heart was not taken;
No, not once, by a one.

I have joked with plenty;
And let laughter fly free.
Not one talk is worth a penny;
Not once you found me.

I have had joy and solace;
With some but not the same.
It just doesn't hold a candle;
Or a match to your flame.

I have felt near to others;
With maybe two scores times three.
But not close to what we have;
Our passion, you and me.

So, believe what I say now;
My search for you is done.
In all of my life,
I have only loved one.

What is it?

What draws me to you,
What keeps me stuck;
What keeps me in your loop?

What keeps me locked inside your path;
What keeps my thoughts on you?

Is it your eyes,
Their lovely shade;
Like honeycombs in their nest.

Is it your drive, the way you push;
To always do your best.

What keeps me locked,
What keeps me steady;
What keeps me standing near?

What keeps me hoping, wanting, wishing;
To never say bye to you, dear?

Could it be your smile,
Could it be your passion;
Could it be your long hair too?

Could it be face that keeps me tangled;
Tongue speaking like a fool?

What is it from you,
That keeps me calm;
That makes me try so hard?

Why is it when you come around:
I suddenly drop my guard.

Could it be the depth,
Of your lovely heart:
That pulls me from the deep?

Could it be the passion of your love;
That makes me want to weep?

I honestly don't know what it is,
And truly, I do not care;

But none have held this spot before;
My heart's all for you, dear.

I Love

I have loved you from the beginning,
And I will love you until the end.
And should you ever need it, dear,
My strength to you I will lend.

I want to grant every wish you have,
And make every dream you've got come true.
I want to spend every hour and minute,
That I have left on earth with you.

I love to see you happy, it's true.
Oh, I love to make you grin.
Whenever you are in my arms,
I see it as a win.

I love holding you tight; I do.
And I cherish holding you close.
I love smelling of your scent, my love,
And I cherish your warmth the most.

I love your head lying on my chest,
I love your hair, all in my face.
I love that it's your place to rest,
Oh, I love your soft embrace.

I love the lipstick stains you leave,
The ones there on my cups.
I love the bumper that you bent,
When you tried to drive my truck.

I love all the things that remind me of you;
The small, big, and all between.
I love the fact that when we're together,
With you, I'm truly seen.

So, all my days, I'll be strong for you,
And I cherish you more each night
And when I lay my head to rest.
I will be thankful that you're mine.

If I could do it again

Someone once asked me,
What I would do;
If I could go back in time,
And sooner find you?

Would I change up the memory,
Of when we first met;
And make it like a movie,
Camera, action, set.

Would I erase the first moment,
Our gazes and paths crossed;
The moment I fell in love,
Cause from site I was lost.

Would I rewrite our history,
And make me more charming?
Would I be more alluring;
Or would it just be alarming?

I knew when we met,
I'd fallen for you.
And from what you told me,
You felt it, too.

Would redoing our meeting,
Change how you felt?
Would retrying that encounter,
Make you look on with doubt?

I think about today
And how we are now.
If I could do it sooner,
I would love to, but how?

Because our first meeting
Was special and true.
And I could never redo,
The day I met you.

The Dream

Dreaming of you;
Behind me today;
We locked eyes for a second;
Then you looked away;

Then, heavy in my chest;
And my soul, I would feel;
A sensation of loss;
For my heart, you would steal;

You'd ask me a question;
To answer that day,
You laid out the options;
Let me choose as I may;

Do I still love you;
Is this really real?
Is what we have true?
What are the feelings I feel?

Then you asked me once more;
This time, hitting true;
Do I live for myself;
Or do I live for you?

Upon waking up,
I stared at the ceiling;
And still felt the dream type of feel I was feeling;

I laid there a while;
And thought about you;
Thought about our future;
And all that we'd do;

But you're not here with me,
You are not close at hand;
So, lying from my bed;
I got up to stand;

The chance of our meeting;
So slim and unique;
And scared was I then;
To not present weak;

I wanted to call you;
And to hear your voice;
To tell you my dream;
And tell you my choice;

For between you and me;
I'd every time choose;
The choice that would always,
Keep me with you.

Secret Smile

Secret Smile you hold in tight.
Secret Smile comes to the light.

Let it shine,
Yes, let it forth.
Let it show,
As true as North.

You hold fast joy;
You keep it locked.
You keep it sealed;
You keep it blocked.

All I wish is to be,
Is the one for you.
Who lets you let go;
And your smile shine through.

Secret Smile you hold in tight.
Secret Smile comes to the light.

Your beautiful face
Is pinched and held;
Yet I can notice,
You start to yield.

Laugh lines creeping up,
So subtly;
Oh, you can't hide them,
No, not from me.

Your smirk comes through,
Your eyes go round;
Yet still you try,
To keep your smile down.

It's cute, I promise;
So unfiltered you.
So, I say again;
Let your smile shine through.

Secret Smile you hold in tight;
Secret Smile comes to the light.

Secret no more,
You let it go;
Now, all can see,
Your radiant glow.

When

When I heard your voice,
For the first time,
I did not know why,
But life changed on a dime.

When I first saw your smile,
I knew it right then.
What I wanted the most,
Was to be on the other end.

When I first felt your touch,
My heart skipped a beat.
And though not understanding,
My heart knew that we'd meet.

When I first heard your laugh,
My soul cried out with glee.
And nothing counted more,
I wanted you with me.

When I first tasted your lips,
My fate was then sealed.
Because with one simple kiss,
All my wounds have been healed.

When I first heard, the three words,
The most important three, you'd say.
I had never been happier,
And I love you too;
Impossibly more each day.

Question

You have freckles across your face,
And hazel flakes in your eyes.
One of them lifts with your smile.
The other widens in your surprise.

Your face, I'm meant to cherish,
Your gentle hands, I'm meant to hold.
Your soft hair, I'm meant to feel,
And so, one knee for you I'll fold.

With your lips, I'm meant to kiss,
And your soul I'm meant to love.
My eyes to you, they wonder,
Your voice is as pure as a dove.

I'll reach into my pocket,
And pull this lovely stone.
And finally, ask the question,
Will you complete my home?

Letters

To the luck I had in meeting you,
To the opportunity of feelings true,
To the victory in life, I'm glad,
To the enduring happiness we've had.

I could

I could listen to you forever;
Hear your voice and all you say.
I could sit there right beside you;
And hope the scene repeats each day.

I could walk right at your shoulder;
I could stand right by your side;
I could be your steady boulder;
And I could be your place to hide.

I could talk about your beauty;
I could talk about your mind;
I could talk on how you're moody;
And I could love still that you're mine.

I could get lost in your presence;
I could lose myself, it's true.
I could love you without pretense;
And I would play the fool for you.

I could scent the sweetest fragrance;
And I would know it's you by smell.
I could point you out if blindfolded;
And I would get it right, no doubt.

I could feel hair soft as silk;
And I would know it's you right then.
And if I hear your distant laughter;
Any sorrow I'd have would mend.

I could live a life without you;
I could live a life love-free.
But honestly, what's the point;
If you're not in this life with me?

If you

If you give me tonight,
I'll give you a memory,
A reflection of what,
The future for us could be.

If you give me the morning,
I'll show you how we'd be together,
Happy in life,
And true through whatever weather.

If you give me the noon time,
Soon as the day goes on,
With each passing hour,
You'll find our bond just as strong.

If you give me the evening,
As the light turns to dark again,
I'll hold you close in my arms,
And we'll pretend the moment won't end.

If you give me the nighttime,
I'll lay beside and keep you safe,
And don't worry about me,
As I'll cherish your warm embrace.

So, if you give me tonight,
And you give me tomorrow,
I'll give you my heart,
And my love with it follows.

To My Future Forever

To my future forever;
I love you here today.
May your life be bright and sunny;
Days hopeful and not gray.

To my future forever;
To the future love of my life.
I promise to hold you firm;
Through all troubles and strife;

To my future forever;
I wish you all the best.
May I soon be right beside you;
Through every future trial and test.

To my future forever;
I'll be waiting for you here.
And here I've been waiting;
Long before I knew it, dear.

To my future forever;
I miss you even now.
Although I do not know you,
My heart knows you still somehow;

To my future forever;
To our forever a night and on.
May you find me one day sooner;
So, we can finally start our song;

To my future forever;
To my future lovely bride.
I promise to cherish you always;
And let love be our guide.

LETTERS OF LONGING.

I Shouldn't

I shouldn't need you,
But need you, I do.
And just because I shouldn't,
Doesn't mean that it's not true.

I shouldn't want you,
Cause for you, I am wrong.
But still, I'm longing for you, dear,
And my heart holds on strong.

I shouldn't cherish you,
But cherish you, I will.
Though it won't change that you're gone,
I'll cherish you each day still.

I shouldn't dream of you,
But those dreams I love the most.
In them, we are a family,
But when I'm awake, you're just a ghost.

No, I shouldn't love you,
But I do though this is true.
And knowing that now, where do I go,
Now that I'm not with you.

About a year

It's been about a year;
Since I last seen you.
And I still sometimes wonder;
What it is right now you do.

Sometimes late at night;
Before I go to sleep.
I remember you next to me;
and my heart for you weeps.

It's been about a year;
Since I last heard your voice.
And still, through all other sounds,
Your melody is my favorite choice.

When I walk into rooms,
I still gaze around for you.
And I know I'm being foolish;
But it's still something that I do.

It's been about a year;
Since I last felt your touch
Your wonderful soft hands;
Your brown hair I love so much.

I can feel the softest silks;
and they don't compare.
I could see the brightest colors;
All less vibrant without you here.

It's been about a year;
Since we shared our last kiss.
And it's not just the action;
But the passion that I miss.

The part of me that cares for you;
That truly loves you still.
Hopes that you'll come back one day;
The other hopes you never will.

So, it's been about a year;
And times been passing by,
I still wish you the best, my dear,
Even if the best is not with I.

Her

Her hazel eyes;
Her sun-tanned skin.
Her long brown hair;
That pulls me in.

Her light, cute laugh;
Her nervous, shy smile.
The way she lingers;
A little longer each while.

She stands up tall;
She holds her head high.
Whenever we speak,
I get lost in her eyes.

Better than perfect;
Her flaws make her shine.
To stand right beside her;
Is the dream that is mine.

One last goodbye;
One last farewell.
And here I stand;
Hollow as a shell.

It was not meant to be;
This thing her and me.
But forever and always;
She'll show in my dreams.

And even though my heart's;
Been torn out and thrown.
I know that I Love her;
Now that I'm alone.

Never would I replace;
The time that we've spent.
Not the summer I fell in Love;
Or the day that we met.

Was It?

Was it nonsense what I felt,
The day we first met?
When you walked into the room,
And just like that, that was it.

The moment that I saw you,
My future came tumbling to.
No longer was I searching;
It was all because of you.

Was it wrong how I felt,
The time we first talked?
You said something crazy;
And my jaw, like my heart, dropped.

I stood there laughing with you;
And when you caught my eye;
We laughed all the more;
I chuckled till I cried.

Was it magic how I felt,
The day we first ran?
Seeing you there flustered;
But determined to try your hand.

I watched in amazement;
The effort you put in;
And I knew that in life,
With that effort, you would win.

Was it bad how I felt;
When we had said goodbye?
You hugged me once and walked away;
And in my heart, I thought I'd die.

As you left, I remembered;
The day you first walked in.
Although it hurt to watch you leave,
I stood right there and grinned.

Was it nonsense how I felt,
The day that we first met?
I guess time will tell;
Cause our story's not done yet.

And so, I will wait for you here;
As I have once waited before.
Only this time now, I know you're out there;
And so, I'll wait for you, mi amor.

If I could

If I could stop loving you tomorrow;
If I could forget the time we've spent.
If I could get you out of my mind;
If I could forget all that you meant.

My life would be much simpler;
Just like a dream, that's true.
And my heart would feel the pain no more;
If I could only not know you.

If I could erase all the memories;
All the loving times we've shared.
Then, the scars would heal right over;
And I'd not think on why they're there.

If I could forget all of the good times;
All the happiness we've had.
Forget the pain of being without you;
I'd have no reason to feel this bad.

If I could pull away the moment;
Of our first loving kiss.
Then there'd be gone the reason;
For me to sit and reminisce.

If I could only go on with living;
And not knowing that you're there.
If I could finally fully sleep at night;
Without you in my prayers.

If I could stop loving you tomorrow;
I'd never take the deal.
I'd relive every joy and pain;
And know my heart won't heal.

For all the time that I've known you,
For every second, minute, day.
I'll hold close to my chest with love;
Until I pass away.

Need To Say

Please look at me,
Don't look away;
And let me say,
What I need to say.

Yes, let me tell;
Let me speak it true;
Of how I feel,
My love for you.

Just let me put it,
Out into the world;
I can no longer keep it,
Buried and furled.

Please stand and listen,
No need to speak;
Hear what I say,
Darling, don't you weep.

For not one more day,
Will I let pass by;
Without telling you,
What I feel inside.

See, I love you truly,
And love you so;
So I'll say it this once,
Before you go.

Through trial and stress,
My heart, you'll have,
It'll always be there,
For you to grab.

For my love won't falter,
My love won't fall;
Know my love goes passed,
The end of all.

Just Say

Just say that you love me,
Just say that it's true,
Just say that you need me,
The way I need you.

Just say that you want me,
Just say that it's so,
Just say that you'll hold me,
And won't let me go.

Just don't be honest with me,
Please tell me the lie.
And I'll pretend I can't see,
Oh, the truth I will hide.

So, say that you love me,
If just for tonight.
And say that you need me,
Even though it's not right.

Please let me have this memory,
This one single thing.
That I can keep forever,
For when you leave this fling.

Where do I go?

Where do I go?
What do I do?
With all this time,
That I am not with you.

How do I wait?
How can I rest?
Awaiting you here,
With my heart out my chest.

Who do I speak to?
What comfort can I find?
Knowing that you're out there,
But we're apart at this time.

What, in the meantime,
Do I do to prepare?
For the next time that we meet,
The next moment we share.

I Want

I want it all, I know I am selfish,
I want you in my life,
But I've been alone so long, it seems,
To change now don't seem right.

I don't want to make concessions at all,
I don't want to give up this ride,
But I also don't want to lose you,
And I want you by my side.

I want to wake up next to you,
And in the shining rays,
The first thing that I see each morning,
Be your amber eyes each day.

I don't want you to leave me here,
Never want to say goodbye,
And I never want to see you tear,
So, my darling, don't you cry.

See the boy in me; he wants it all,
No allowances in between,
He's stuck in me, he cannot see,
The reality through the dream.

But the man in me, he knows, he does,
Just what he still must do,
Giveaway his current pleasures now,
And prepare himself for you.

For there's one longing held inside myself,
Above every other wish,
It's to be with you, forever on,
And for that dream, I will not risk.

I will not risk a day, I will not risk an hour,
No, not a minute or second will lapse,
I will not take the chance of losing you,
For your love, I'll close all gaps.

For every breath with you is a wish come true,
And every night a heavenly dream,
And so, I'll make the changes needed for you,
To keep your heart with me.

Out of reach

So far out of reach,
So far out of hand,
So far from my sight,
So far from my land.

I wish I could see you.
I wish I could hold you.
I wish I could keep you.
I wish I was more bold too.

So far out of reach,
So far out of hand,
So far from my grasp,
So far, I can't stand.

I'll wait for you here;
And wait, I will do.
I'll wait our next meeting;
And wait to see you.

So far out of reach,
So far out of hand,
So far from my side,
So far from our plan.

So, love you, I will.
So, love you, I do.
So, love you for always.
Til forever is through.

So, not out of heart,
So, not out of plan,
So, not out of reach,
So, not out of hand.

Goodbye Dear

When I look into your eyes,
I see forever staring back at me;
And it's painfully hard to know,
That what I want for us, Will never be.

Yet I'll be thankful still that fate,
Has crossed our paths in life.
And seeing you will always,
Be my boon in its own right.

I honestly am happy now,
Simply having had met you;
And I'll look back fondly on it all,
Remembering all the things we'd do.

You weren't just beautiful,
You were also true,
You were wise in your outlooks,
And unapologetically you.

And just seeing you be,
Existing as you were;
With all your passionate drive,
And all the feelings you'd stir.

It made me want to grow
And made me want to learn;
To be a better man in life,
And let my doubts away burn.

I want to be somebody,
Who is truly worthy of you,
And even though it won't happen,
It still helps me push on through.

So, I will say this here,
And I will utter this truth,
For the rest of my life,
I will always thank you.

For no matter who I meet,
Or who's love I should have,
They will now meet the person,
You have pulled from the ash.

No matter where I go,
No matter who I see,
If they like who I am now,
It's because you have changed me.

You were the bread that helped feed me,
The breath that gave me life,
You were water when I was thirsty,
You were my shelter in the night.

You were the perfect shade in sunlight,
A cool breeze by the beach,
You were the match that lit my torchlight,
A star so close yet out of reach.

And even though I know I lost you,
Now that you're far away,
My feelings of admiration,
Will forever for you stay.

You were the person that I needed.
At the right place, in the right time,
Maybe not for romance,
But for this building character of mine.

I will always be your biggest fan,
And I'll always cheer you on,
I'll always wish your nights are good,
And that your troubles won't last long.

There are a hundred more things that I wish to say,
but I guess I'll leave off here.
So, I'll say this one last thing to you,
I love you; goodbye, dear.

You Said

You said life was beauty,
And you said love was pure.
That our connection was captivating,
That our love will endure.

So, I'll hold on forever,
To what I know is done.
And the memories I treasure,
They will stay when you're gone.

Maybe the pain of being without you,
Won't ever cease or ebb.
Maybe I'll suffer into insanity,
While I keep you in my head.

But I'll hold on tight to this necklace,
To this gift you gave to me.
And I'll wear around my neck each day,
Out plain where all can see.

I will not separate our moments,
Our shared times, good or bad.
But I'll hide away my misery,
And for your new life, I'll be glad.

You once told me life is beauty,
And I believe it to my soul.
You once asked me to hold on forever,
So, in my heart, I won't let go.

And yes, our connection, it was captivating,
And yes, I know your heart was pure.
And though you've parted ways from me,
My love for you will endure.

One thing

I think that you are beautiful;
Each and every way.
And if I had one sentence to speak,
It'd be what I would say.

You opened up my horizons.
And brought back what was lost.
You did it never knowing;
Purchased my love all at no cost.

I don't know what it was about you;
That made my heart turn on.
What I know is a simple thing;
That I've never felt so strong.

I hope sometimes you think of me;
As I still think of you.
And should we never cross paths again,
I'm still thankful you passed through.

I Will

I will let you go now, my love,
I will let you leave my life,
I will stand and watch you walk away,
Bear the pain, the sorrow, and strife.

I will let you change, and I will let you grow,
I will let you be free again,
I will no longer hold back the person you are.
And when you are gone, happiness, I'll pretend.

I will bear it all and fake a smile,
So, your joy can flow on through,
I will hold at bay, keep the sorrow away,
And try to be happy for you

I hope one day a time will pass,
Where for me happiness is true,
But the thing that I fear the most,
Is I'll not fall out of love, with you.

Memories

I'll keep you in my heart and soul;
And keep it locked away.
Regret that I will never say;
The things I want to say.

I'll love you from afar, I must;
To keep you truly free.
Knowing what I wish for us,
Will surely never be.

Still happy just knowing that;
You're happy all the same.
I'll take our memories and love;
And let you forget my name.

Cause loss of love so pure and strong;
I'd not wish you to feel as I.
I'd rather keep away all the pain;
Then, ever see you cry.

So, forget me now, forget me soon;
And I'll forget you not.
And while I fade from memory,
I'll reap what I had wrought.

Leave me in the morning

You'll leave me in the morning;
You'll leave me hanging on.
I'll wake up in the daytime;
And in the daytime, you'll be gone.

You'll leave me in the morning,
But the mornings still far off.
So, hold me tight in your arms,
And rock me strong and soft.

Keep me in your memories,
When you are far away.
And know, my dear, that always,
I'll wish that you had stayed.

So, leave me in the morning,
If that is what you must.
But know that you are always,
The one that I loved most.

You'll leave me in the morning,
You'll leave me hanging on.
And you'll take part of me;
And my soul when you are gone.

Yes, you'll leave me in the morning,
You'll leave me hanging on.
Yes, you'll take part of me;
And my soul when you are gone.

Leave you in the morning

I'll leave you in the morning,
I'll leave you all alone.
I'll leave you in the morning,
And march away from home.

But tonight, we are together,
And memories we'll make.
And when I leave you morning time,
My heart and soul will break.

I'll leave you in the daytime,
When the morning rays shine through.
But tonight, my dear, it's all about;
The love I have for you.

I'll leave you in the morning,
Because that is what I must.
And your memory I'll carry,
Till my bodies turn to dust.

So, I'll leave you in the morning,
And I hope you don't forget.
Everything that we've shared,
Since the day that we had met.

I'll leave you in the morning,
And your life will still go on.
And there will come a day, my dear,
When you will meet someone,

And if you could remember,
The feelings that we shared.
Just think of me fondly,
And the love you once had there.
Yes, think of me fondly;
And the love we once had shared.

LETTERS OF FAMILY, FRIENDS, & LOSS.

Grey

Your eyes have gone foggy;
Your fur has turned gray.
You still run in your dreams;
But can't run in the day.

Your legs just don't work;
Like how they used to do.
Back feet held close together;
And they shake a little, too.

But you still get up and greet me;
Every time that I come home.
And you still give me comfort;
And don't judge me when I'm wrong.

You sleep a lot more nowadays;
And your energies gone down.
But you still like exploring;
Seeing new things to be found.

You've moved around a lot with me;
Across cities and states, too.
You see my growth throughout the years;
And you've helped me push on through.

Your breath is deep and heavy now;
And your teeth are almost gone.
But you're still a baby in my eyes;
And on you, I'll spoil and fawn.

Your eyes have gone foggy now;
And your fur, it's turned gray.
But I still love my good ol' boy;
Until forever and a day.

                Dedicated to:
                My Dog, Geronimo.

Mama

I remember your laugh,
I remember your voice,
I remember the way you hugged me.

I remember your smile,
I remember your eyes,
And I remember how you loved me.

I remember your hair,
I remember your hands,
I remember how they'd hold me.

I remember your smell,
I remember your dresses,
And how your room was always comfy.

You cooked the best food,
Made the coziest blankets,
And gave the best hugs, too.

And I can't put into letters,
All the trials I would better,
If I could once again, see you.

You had never got to see,
the person I've come to be,
The person you helped mold out.

I was a kid when you passed,
Went from granite straight to glass,
Oh, I was then broken, without a doubt.

It was then that I'd feel,
The full pain of sorrow real,
And let grief out with a cry.

And while time has moved on,
I'll still morn that you're gone,
And I'll never say goodbye.

I'll hold your memory in,
No longer cry; I will grin,
I will cherish the memories I have.

There'll be no more to make,
So, I'll keep what I can take,
And reminisce on what I've grabbed.

I know I'll see you again,
And I'll love you to the end,
So, Mama, I'll see you up above.

But I must wait for a while,
Though, as I wait, I will smile,
Because even now, I feel your love.

Papa

Strong as an ox,
And a stubborn as one, too.
I learned how to be a man,
It was all because of you.

You took care of the family,
Took care of the bills.
You ate the expired food,
And gave us the new meals.

You didn't complain about work,
Or the struggles you had to face.
You kept your head held up high,
Showed me to go through trial with Grace.

You fixed the things that needed fixing,
And you worked without being asked.
You loved my Mama, there was no doubt,
I only saw you cry when she passed.

You taught me about money,
You taught me to be tough,
You taught me to be funny,
You taught me that life was rough.

You never let me give excuses,
And you never let me give up.
You made sure my word was worth its uses,
You kept me from going corrupt.

I looked up to you then,
And I still do today.
Superman till the end,
And every night, I will pray.

To be Strong as an ox,
And a stubborn as one, too.
Because I learned how to be a man,
And it was all because of you.

Still holding On

I'm still holding on,
To everything I've done with you.
I'm still keeping strong,
To memories of all we'd do.

Goodbye is hard;
When the truth is just not setting on.
It's tough to miss;
What I do not accept as gone.

I'm still holding to our past;
No, I can't let it go.
I'm still grasping hard,
but the truth is seeping in, though slow.

If goodbye forever,
Is what I must say to you.
Then let it be tomorrow,
For when the light of day is new.

I'm still holding on,
To every memory and wish.
I still haven't given you,
My last hug or kiss.

I look up above,
While you sit and look down at me.
I sit still by this stone,
And think on how we used to be.

I'm still holding tight,
And I'm still holding true to you.
I'll talk for hours on end,
And speak on, like we used to do.

There may come a moment,
And a day when time will pass,
That I'll remember you,
Longer than I've known you last.

But I'm still holding on,
And I'm still clinging tight it's true,
So, when my time it comes,
I can be again with you.

Farewell

Goodbye now, my friend,
Farewell, one last time,
The last time I saw you,
Will not be the last time you saw I.

Rest easy now, my friend,
Sleep, peaceful forever on,
You once told me the trick of remembrance,
Is for a person to die young.

Lay peaceful now, my friend,
All your hardships are finally through,
You lived a good life down here,
And just know we all miss you.

So goodbye once again, my friend,
Farewell, one last time,
And grateful I'll always be,
That your path had crossed mine.

My memories

I woke up today and saw the dawn,
I woke up, remembered, and swore.
I guess it's still a part of me,
Every day, it claims me a little more.

So, I did the task I set ahead,
I did the hard job first.
And with time to spare,
I didn't stop there,
I worked on it like a curse.

I can't sit around,
Or I'll ponder too much,
And I'll think about this life.
For it seems to me most cannot see,
Life's beauty through all its strife.

So, as I work, I'll reminisce,
On all the people that I've met.
I'll remember who they were back then,
Oh, I'll try not to forget.

The nice, the good, the funny, and grand,
All the people from my past.
The great and stoic,
Both normal and heroic,
Memories like looking through glass.

I won't forget, as I grow old,
I won't let time take it from me,
My hearing may go,
My site may leave,
But my memories will always be.

Friends

We have aged on here, my friend;
Old men now, me and you.
Yet, as we sit and talk again,
I feel as if we're new.

We joke and laugh and reminisce;
About the good times long and passed.
We sit, and then we ponder on;
How had time flown so fast?

There was a time, so long ago;
When we were once young men.
It's funny just to think about;
How we were once back then.

We had no memories to speak of;
No times we've had together.
And yet we reconciled that fact;
Staying true through every weather.

I've seen you at the best of times;
And you've seen me at my worst.
I saw you on your wedding day;
And you'll see me in my hearse.

We sit and joke and laugh around;
And to everyone nearby.
We're just a couple of old men;
So, no one bats an eye.

We've been to war, to hell and back;
Both figuratively and for true.
We've seen each other at our lowest;
And we pushed each other through.

And as the years they come and pile on;
And our hair thins and turns gray.
We laugh about the good old times;
And won't trade a single day.

Time

It was war that brought us together.
It was time that tore us apart.
It was brotherhood we ended in.
It was strangers how we'd start.

We were boys, young and youthful;
Ready to fight our cause.
It was reality that set in truthful;
That made us stop and pause.

We were soldiers once and young;
As General Hel Moore once said.
And young still are our brothers;
Who rest eternal in their bed.

It was honor, duty, and loyalty;
That made us fight the beast.
It was horror, gore, and bloodshed;
That made us wish for peace.

And those of us who remember;
Those of us still around.
Carry with us the ember;
Of where freedoms cost is found.

And we'd do it again if, once more;
Just so that the ones we love;
Won't ever have to question their place;
With the one that stands above.

LETTERS OF FAITH.

Follow

You have guided me when I was lost,
Cut me loose when I was bound.
And when my life was turned and tossed,
At my weakest, you'd be found.

You had pieced me back together,
And made me stronger still.
And now I'm lighter than a feather,
Because your love for me, I feel.

You carried me at my lowest,
You guided me through the dark.
You protected me, I know this,
In my life, I see your mark.

You walked there right beside me,
Through every trial I faced.
When I could not see you guiding me,
You still saved me with your grace.

You forgave me for my weakness,
Even though you didn't have to.
You pulled me from the bleakness,
You help me push on though.

You have been here right beside me,
Since the day my life began.
And no matter what trials I'll see,
With you, I will always stand.

Faith

I have never denied,
What I knew to be true;
But here, as I sit,
I contemplate you;

I realize now,
I haven't always kept faith.
I'd live for tomorrow,
Not the sabbath but the eighth.

I'd always just assumed,
That I'd have more time.
Wake up one day,
And be righteous on a dime.

But righteous is something,
That never I'd be.
For the sins of the Father;
And mine rest upon me.

One day, I'd pick up,
The good book and read.
One day, I'd finally,
Let faith plant its seed.

But always tomorrow,
I'd put off the day.
Then tomorrow would come,
And then pass away.

I always assumed,
I just had it right.
That faith was so simple,
Not something I'd fight.

Then, older I got,
And simple no more.
For my faith was tested,
By the world at my door.

The bad and the ugly,
How can this be?
If I can't abide it,
Then how could he?

While answers are not,
Easy to come.
I opened the book
And beginning I start from.

And truly, the world,
Is a different place.
When I've read his words,
And feel his grace.

Heavy is the head;
His crown sits upon.
And terrible is it,
That from him we have gone.

And while I'll never,
Truly know his will;
I go to my knees,
And pray to him still.

For comfort and solace,
In his presence, I know;
And when my time comes,
To him, I will go.

The Path

Lying alone,
This time, and I see.
The fate that God,
Has set before me.

Stumbling, tripping,
Each time that I walk.
Knowing that God,
He just wants to talk.

I stand, I turn,
I run, trying to flee.
For I did not want,
What's coming to be.

The Lord comes down,
The savior of men.
Grabbing me tight,
Holding my right hand.

Lifting me up,
With one simple touch.
Why was it I,
Who's pulled from the bunch?

With one simple stroke,
My life, I was shown.
But why is it I,
Must leave from my home?

The path I was shown
That God gave to me;
Does not leave me home
But home, I will see.

And so, I will rest,
And sleep in this bed.
Lying alone,
I'll lay down my head.

I know in the end,
Where my path will lead.
To my savior and maker,
Through him, I am freed.

I See

I see the bluest skies,
I see the greenest trees,
I see the world for what it is,
And what it could be.

I see the darkest of oceans,
I see the clearest of lakes,
I see the brightest of flowers,
I see the leaves fall in flakes.

I see the whiteness of winter,
I see the softest of snow,
I see the plants as they wither,
I see them once again grow.

I see the birds in the sky,
I see the deer on the land,
I see the squirrels running by,
I see the fox as they plan.

I see the darkness of night,
I see the brightness of day,
I see the dusks fading light,
I see the dawn's shining rays.

I see the love of a mother,
I see the strength of a dad,
I see the mischief of a brother,
I see a sister's caring hand.

I see those who are great,
I see those who are false,
I see those who are winning,
I see those who are lost.

I see the world build-up,
I see time passing by,
I see that babies are born,
I see that people, they die.

I see life for what it is,
And what it should be,
So, we must make the best,
Of our time, you and me.

* * * * * * * * * * * *

About the Author

Hi there; my name is Elijah Chavez. I guess this is where I write a little bit about myself. I'm originally from Southern California, more specifically, the city of La Puente. I left home at eighteen when I enlisted as an Infantryman in the U.S. Army. Since then, I have had the honor of meeting some of the best people I have ever met in my life. Writing was never something I'd ever thought of doing. Especially considering I had not graduated from high school. Nevertheless, here I am. Once I started, I found out I quite enjoyed it, and so that's how these works came about. I sincerely hope you have enjoyed at least some of them.

* * * * * * * * * * * *

Printed in the USA
CPSIA information can be obtained
at www.ICGtesting.com
CBHW030414190724
11796CB00009B/303